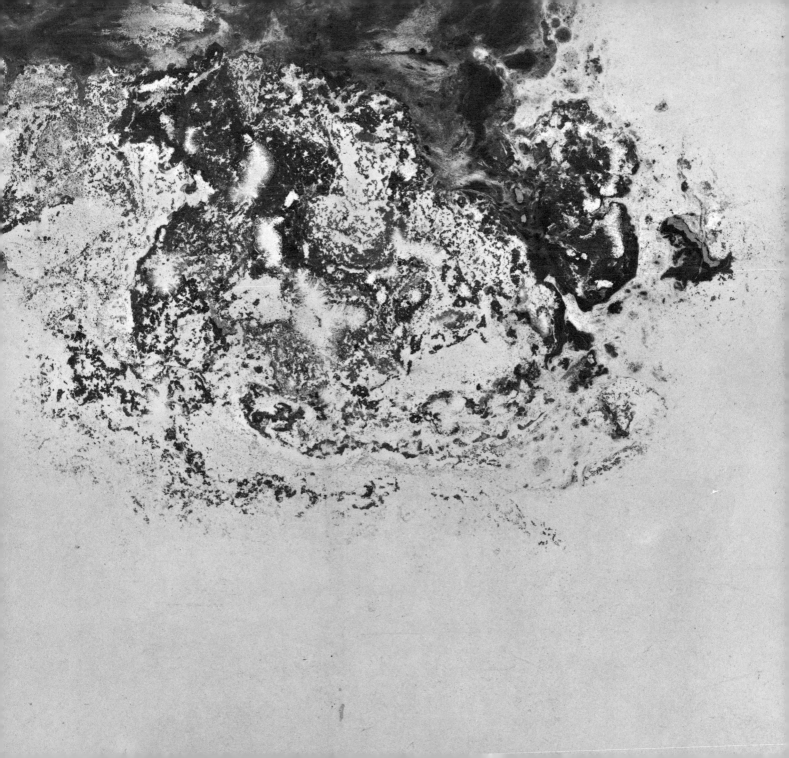

God Is In The Mountain

God Is In The Mountain

Selected and illustrated by Ezra Jack Keats

Holt, Rinehart and Winston   New York   Chicago   San Francisco

This is a collection of voices and intimations.
They speak to us from different times and different places.
What they have in common is the awareness of a dimension
without which life is indeed meaningless.

I should like to share these glimpses into the Way offered us—
beautiful and potent, within us and around us, ever present and waiting.
E.J.K.

God Is In The Mountain

I am in every religion as a thread
through a string of pearls.

HINDUISM

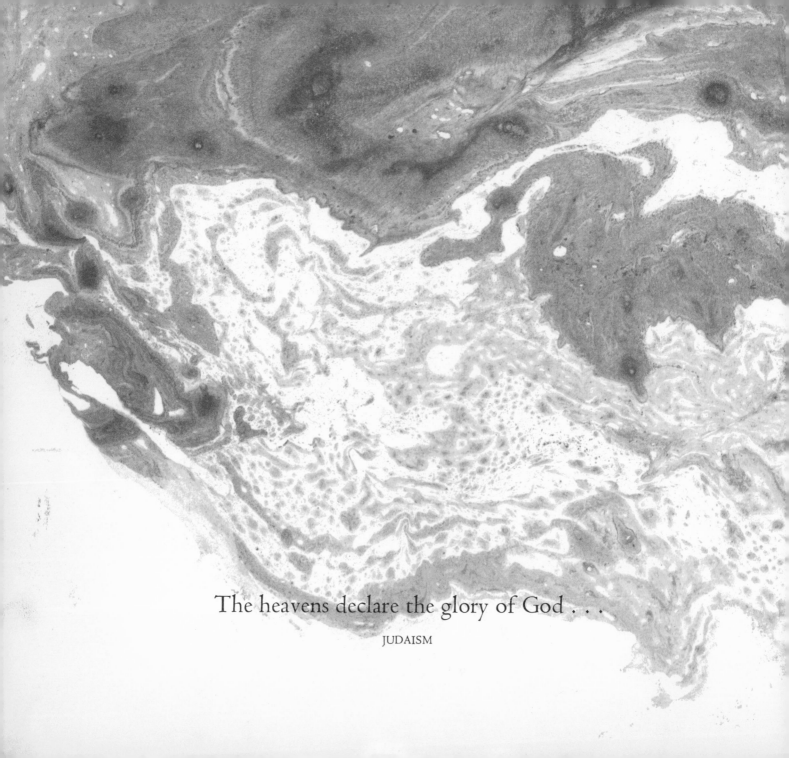

The heavens declare the glory of God . . .

JUDAISM

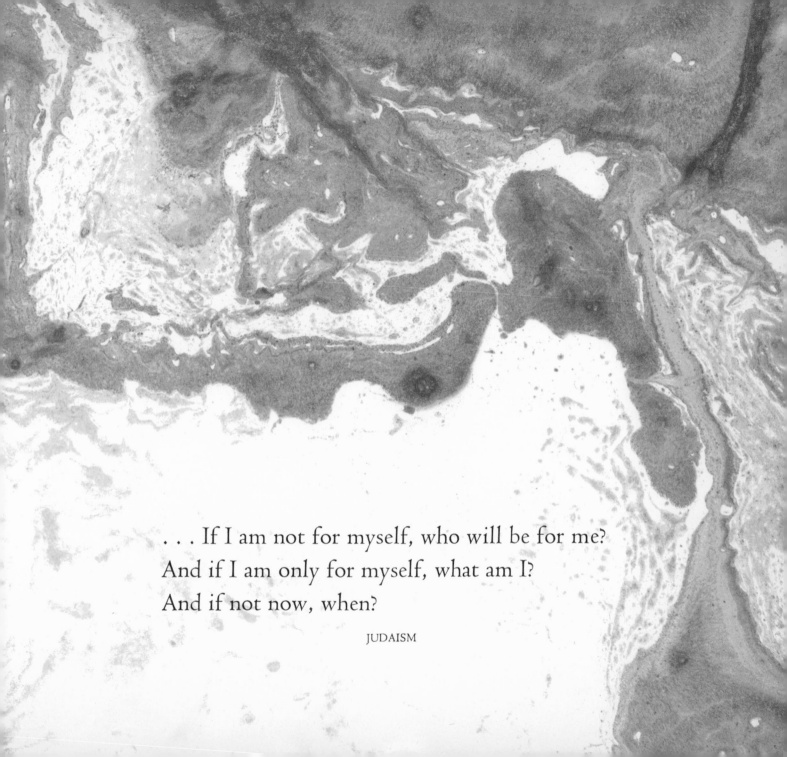

. . . If I am not for myself, who will be for me?
And if I am only for myself, what am I?
And if not now, when?

JUDAISM

There are ways but the Way is uncharted . . .

TAOISM

The feet can walk; let them walk.
The hands can hold; let them hold.
Hear what is heard by your ears;
see what is seen by your eyes. . . .

TAOISM

. . .weave for us a garment of brightness;
May the warp be the white light of morning,
May the weft be the red light of evening,
May the fringes be the falling rain,
May the border be the standing rainbow.
Thus weave for us a garment of brightness,
That we may walk fittingly where birds sing,
That we may walk fittingly where grass is green,
O our Mother the Earth, O our Father the Sky.

AMERICAN INDIAN

Are you less than a piece of earth?
When a piece of earth finds a friend, that is, the spring,
it gains a hundred thousand flowers.

ISLAM

No kind of beast is there on earth
nor fowl that flieth with its wings,
but is a folk like you . . .

ISLAM

God is in the water, God is in the dry land,
God is in the heart, God is in the forest,
God is in the mountain, God is in the cave.

SIKHISM

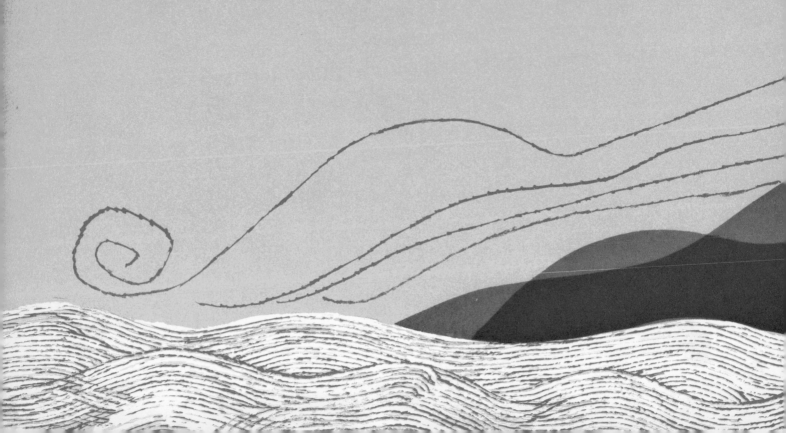

Being beautiful one should not be charmed by it:
it is the light of the Lord, that shines in all bodies.

SIKHISM

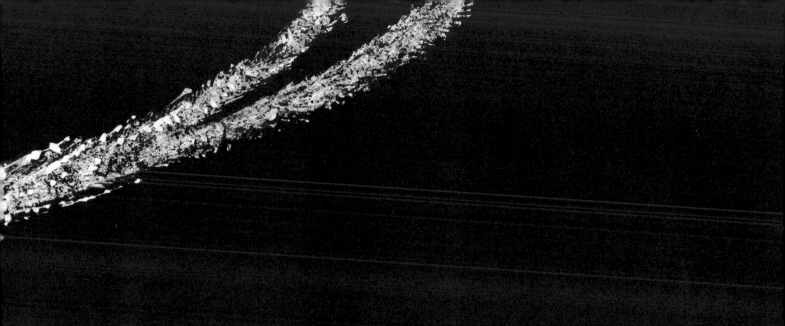

I am like the quetzal bird,
I am created in the one and only God;
I sing sweet songs among the flowers;
I chant songs and rejoice in my heart.

AZTEC

. . .If two make peace with each other in this one house,
they shall say to the mountain:
"Be moved," and it shall be moved.

CHRISTIANITY

Consider the lilies of the field, how they grow;
they toil not, neither do they spin:
and yet I say unto you, that even Solomon in all his glory
was not arrayed like one of these.

CHRISTIANITY

He who is the Self in man,
and he who is the Self in the sun,
are one.

HINDUISM

What is within us is also without.
What is without is also within.
He who sees difference between
what is within and what is without
goes evermore from death to death.

HINDUISM

All ye under the heaven!
Regard heaven as your father, earth as your mother,
and all things as your brother and sisters.

SHINTOISM

The power of spiritual forces in the Universe —
how active it is everywhere!
Invisible to the eyes and impalpable to the senses,
it is inherent in all things,
and nothing can escape its operation.

CONFUCIANISM

The opportunity that God sends
does not wake up him who is asleep.

AFRICAN

Talking with one another
is loving one another.

AFRICAN

Every divine word has come into existence
through the heart's thought and tongue's command.

EGYPTIAN

. . .And from the shining stream of rain the trees
Perfect their fruits. Joint cause of all am I.

GREEK

Mortal though I be, yea ephemeral, if but a moment
I gaze up to the night's starry domain of heaven,
Then no longer on earth I stand; I touch the Creator,
And my lively spirit drinketh immortality.

GREEK

Do you not seek a light,
ye who are surrounded by darkness?

BUDDHISM

Stars, darkness, a lamp, a phantom, dew, a bubble.
A dream, a flash of lightning, and a cloud—
thus we should look upon the world.

Ezra Jack Keats is the distinguished author-illustrator of THE SNOWY DAY, for which he was awarded the 1963 Caldecott Medal, WHISTLE FOR WILLIE, JOHN HENRY: *An American Legend*, and JENNIE'S HAT. In addition, he has recently illustrated a collection of Haiku compiled by Richard Lewis, entitled IN A SPRING GARDEN.

Mr. Keats, who has been interested in art since childhood, and taught himself to draw, has been commissioned to do a set of five cards for the 1966 UNICEF Christmas selection.

Mr. Keats was born in Brooklyn and now resides in New York City.

Grateful acknowledgment is made to the following publishers and authors for permission to reprint copyrighted material:

Behrman House, Inc., for the following selection reprinted from SAYINGS OF THE FATHERS by Joseph H. Hertz, published by Behrman House, Inc., 1261 Broadway, New York 1, New York. ("If I am not for myself, who will be for me?" — Hillel)

E. J. Brill Ltd. for the following selection from THE GOSPEL ACCORDING TO THOMAS, ed. A. Guillaumont, H. -Ch. Puech, G. Quispel and W. Till and Yassah 'Abd al-Masih, E. J. Brill, 1959, Leiden. ("If two make peace with each other in this one house" — Jesus)

The Clarendon Press, Oxford, for the following selections from THE OXFORD BOOK OF GREEK VERSE IN TRANSLATION, ed. Higham and Bowra. ("And from the shining stream of rain..." — Aeschylus; "Mortal though I be..." — Ptolemaeus)

The estate of Dr. S. G. Champion for the following selections from READINGS FROM WORLD RELIGIONS by S. G. Champion and Dorothy Short, reprinted by permission of Mrs. B. C. Briault. ("Being beautiful one should not be charmed by it..." — Arjan; "God is in the water, God is in the dry land..." — Gobino Sinah; "Are you less than a piece of earth?" — Mishkat-el-Massabih; "No kind of beast is there on earth..." — Qur'an; "The heavens declare the glory of God..." — Psalms of David; "Stars, darkness, a lamp, a phantom..." — The Vagrakkhedika; "Consider the lilies of the field..." — Jesus; "The feet can walk, let them walk..." — Chuang-Tzu; "When the sky is clear..." — Oracle at a Tajima Shrine; "All ye under heaven..." — Oracle of the Deity Atsuta)

Harper and Row, Inc., for the following selections from THE CHOICE IS ALWAYS OURS by D. B. Phillips. ("Do you not seek a light..." — The Dhammapada; "I am in every religion..." — Bhagavad-Gita)

The New American Library and W. T. Stace for the following selection from THE TEACH-INGS OF THE MYSTICS by W. T. Stace, reprinted by permission of the author. ("There are ways but the Way is uncharted." — Lao-Tzu)

The New American Library and the Vedanta Society of Southern California for the follow-ing selections from the Prabhavananda-Manchester THE UPANISHADS, copyright by the Vedanta Society of California. ("What is within us is also without..." — Katha; "He who is the Self in man..." — Taittiriya)

The Peter Pauper Press for the following selections from AFRICAN PROVERBS by C. and W. Leslau. ("The opportunity that God sends..."; "Talking with one another...")

G. P. Putnam's Sons and Coward-McCann for the following selections from AMERICAN INDIAN PROSE AND POETRY by Margot Astrow, copyright 1946 by Margot Astrow. ("I am like the quetzal bird..." — A song by Nezahualcoyotl; "Weave for us a garment of bright-ness..." — Tewa)

The Viking Press, Inc. and Russell and Volkening, Inc. for the following selection from THE MASKS OF GOD—ORIENTAL MYTHOLOGY, copyright © 1962 by Joseph Campbell. Re-printed by permission of the author. ("Every divine word has come into existence...")

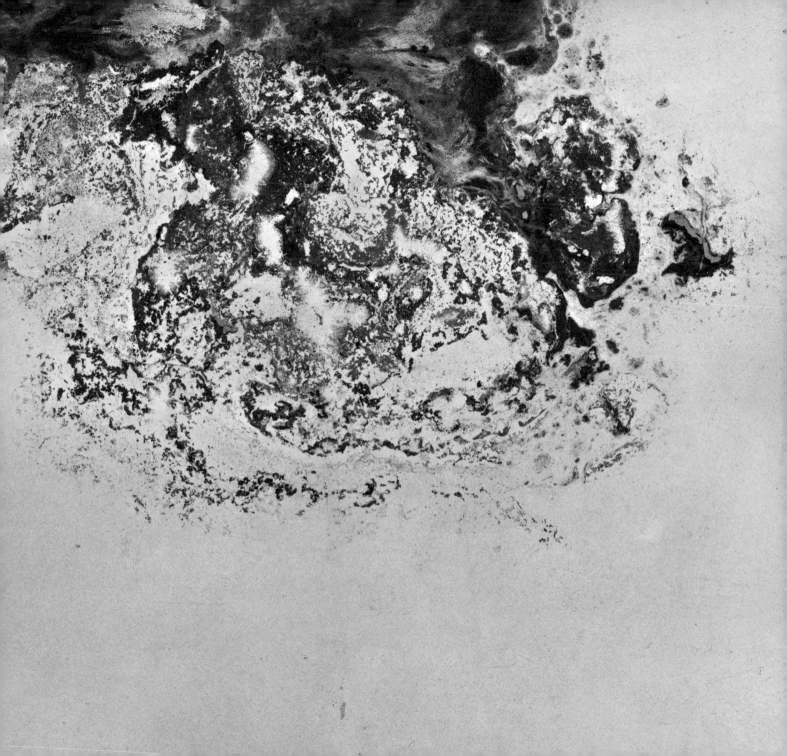